He Healed Them

The Church's Ministry of Healing

By
Dr. Frank Bateman Stanger

First Fruits Press
Wilmore, Kentucky
c2013

ISBN: 9781621711162

He Healed Them: The Church's Ministry of Healing By Frank Bateman
Stanger
First Fruits Press, © 2013, Asbury Seminary Press, [196-]

Digital version at http://place.asburyseminary.edu/
firstfruitsheritagematerial/68/

Stanger, Frank Bateman.
    "He healed them" : the church's ministry of healing / by Frank Bateman
    Stanger.
    iii, 24 p. ; 21 cm.
    Wilmore, Ky. : First Fruits Press, c2013.
    Reprint. Previously published: Wilmore, Ky. : Asbury Seminary Press,
    [196-].
    ISBN: 9781621711162 (pbk.)
    1. Spiritual healing. 2. Church work with the sick. I. Title
    BT732.5 .S83 2013   234.131
Cover design by Haley Hill

asburyseminary.edu
800.2ASBURY
204 North Lexington Avenue
Wilmore, Kentucky 40390

First Fruits
THE ACADEMIC OPEN PRESS OF ASBURY SEMINARY

He Healed Them

The Church's Ministry of Healing

By
Dr. Frank Bateman Stanger

Asbury Seminary Press
Wilmore, Kentucky 40390

Contents

. . . .

Preface
· · · · · · · · ·

For seven years Dr. Frank Bateman Stanger, President of Asbury Theological Seminary, Wilmore, Kentucky, has edited the page of The Herald, "He Healed Them." Many letters have come to my desk, along with hundreds of personal testimonies given me in the course of my travels over the nation, expressing deep gratitude and appreciation for the benefits received from this page. We have also had numerous requests for some of the materials in this special feature of The Herald, in booklet form.

It is at the request of the editorial committee of The Herald that Dr. Stanger has given the "Pitcher of Cream" on the church ministry of healing in this convenient booklet format. The booklet is available without cost to new subscribers to The Herald. It is also available without cost to present subscribers who send in a gift subscription.

This little classic on healing centers around The Great Physician, the source of all healing.

J.C. McPheeters, Editor

What Do We Mean by Healing?

· · · · · · · · ·

The Church's ministry of healing rests fundamentally upon the nature of man, as created by God, in His own image. Man has been created as a unity. The basic components of his nature — spirit, mind, and body — are distinct entities and are interrelated, and together they comprise a personality, which ideally is characterized by unity. Man fulfills the potential of his creation only as the various parts of his personality work in harmonious balance and affect each other constructively.

The Church's ministry of healing is concerned with the health of man as a total person. Two definitions of healing are particularly helpful. Leslie D. Weatherhead defines healing as "the process of restoring the broken harmony which prevents human personality at any point of body, mind or spirit from its perfect functioning in its relevant environment; that is, the body in the material world; the mind in the realm of true ideas; and the spirit in its relationship to God."

Bernard Martin speaks of the healing of man as "a liberation from physical, mental and spiritual shackles which prevent him from reaching the full maturity of a man destined for eternal life."

A careful study of these definitions reveals several important truths about healing. First of all, healing relates to normalcy within human personality. Healing has as its objective the making possible of the normal functioning of the person on the highest level of being. Weatherhead speaks of "restoring the broken harmony." Martin speaks of "a liberation from shackles, which prevent maturity."

In the second place, healing relates to every aspect of the human personality — body, mind, and spirit. Healing is concerned with wholeness for the total person. Sometimes the basic need of a person is for physical healing. At other times the basic need is mental and emotional. Again the basic need is often spiritual. Perhaps there are fundamental needs in more than one area of human personality. Or there may be the need for the harmonious working of all the component parts of the human personality.

There is a third truth: healing is usually a process. However, this is not meant to exclude either instantaneous healing or instantaneous acts of faith, which initiate healing.

Finally, healing is always related to functional aims. Healing is never effected for purposes of self-display or even primarily for verbal witnessing. Healing is never to be sought merely as another miracle which the omnipotent God delights to toss about. Rather healing always relates to the "perfect functioning" of the person. The New Testament concept of "perfect" always includes Divine purposefulness. Healing makes possible not only activity in the name of Jesus Christ, but also maturity of being in Christ.

Let it be kept in mind that healing power belongs to God. Medicine does not heal. Doctors and surgeons do not heal. Psychiatric therapies do not heal. Rest does not heal. Climate does not heal. God only uses these means and agents of healing. All healing is of God.

These words of the eminent French doctor, Ambroise Pare, are inscribed over the gateway of the College of Surgeons in Paris — "I dressed the patient's wounds; God healed him." Over the entrance to the Columbia-Presbyterian Medical Center in New York City are these words — "For from the Most High cometh healing."

Five Facts that are Compelling
· · · · · · · · ·

Out of my studies and experiences and participation in the Church's ministry of healing have emerged Five Compelling Facts. These five facts are logically-deducted, Scripturally-oriented, relevantly-documented and hence irrefutable, as far as I am concerned. Let us, therefore, consider these Five Compelling Facts.

Fact 1
· · · · ·

The first fact that is compelling is that Jesus, as a religious leader, inaugurated a ministry of healing. A study of the Gospel records reveals that Jesus devoted much of His ministry to healing. Most of His miracles were miracles of healing. In the Gospels, there are records of at least twenty-six healing miracles, which Jesus performed upon individuals. There are five other references to His healing ministry in respect to "a great multitude," "many people," and "others."

A medical classification has been made of the healing miracles of Jesus and it is pointed out that He healed the following known ailments: fever, malaria, leprosy, congenital blindness, Parkinson's disease, nephritis, arthritis, fibroids of the uterus or functional hemorrhage, epilepsy, deafness, blindness, crippledness, and insanity. And certainly Jesus must also have encountered such symptoms as fear, anxiety, insomnia, nervousness, palpitation, heat disorder, indigestion, excitement, and depression.

When Jesus sent forth His disciples, he instructed them, among other things, to heal the sick. "And when He had called unto Him His twelve disciples, He gave them power against unclean spirits, to cast them out, and to heal all manner of sickness and all manner of disease." "Jesus... commanded them, 'And as ye go, preach, saying, the kingdom of heaven is at hand. Heal the sick, cleanse the lepers, raise the dead, cast out devils: freely ye have received, freely give,'" (Matthew 10:1, 5, 7, 8).

As the earthly ministry of Jesus was drawing to a close, He told His disciples that "He that believeth on me, the works that I do shall he do also; and greater works than these shall he do," (John 14:12). And what were these works, which Jesus had done? Among them were works of healing.

Fact 2
.....

A second fact that is compelling is that healing was a regular ministry in the Early Christian Church. There are at least fourteen records of healing in the Books of the Acts. These included the healing of fever and other illnesses, the casting out of unclean spirits, the healing of the lame and paralyzed, and the dead being raised to life.

In 1 Corinthians 12:9, 29, 30, Paul asserts that the gift of healing is one of the gifts of the Spirit that has been given to the church "for the common good."

James, in his epistle (5:13, 14, 15), gives interesting instructions to the sick concerning prayers for healing. "Is any among you afflicted? Let him pray…Is any sick among you? Let him call for the elders of the church; and let them pray over him, anointing him with oil in the name of the Lord: and the prayer of faith shall save the sick, and the Lord shall raise him up…"

The New Testament writers often related the health of the body to the grace of God. "For this cause many are weak and sickly among you," (1 Corinthians 11:30), "the body for the Lord and the Lord for the body," (1 Corinthians 6:13), "I wish above all things that thou mayest prosper and be in health, even as thy should prospereth," (3 John 2).

Anyone interested in studying healing in the Early Church should read Evelyn Frost's book, entitled Christian Healing. The author has made a study of the writings of the Church Fathers, from Clement in 95 A.D. to Lactantius around 300 A.D. The writings of the Early Church Fathers speak for themselves and show conclusively that it was the regular thing for the Church between the time of Jesus and the official adoption of religion by the Roman Empire to carry on a healing ministry. The Early Christians preached; they taught; they also healed. Now Evelyn Frost suggests something which is very illuminating when she asks: "Could it be that when ecclesiasticism began to enter the Church, interest in the spiritual ministry of healing began to diminish?" Let me add: Is it possible to substitute the clanging of the ecclesiastical machinery for the sound of the winds of the Spirit of God? And could it be that spiritual ministries of healing do not thrive very well in climates of ecclesiasticism?

Fact 3
. . . . .

The third fact that is compelling is so extensive in its implications that it will be possible to deal with it only in a very general sense within the limits of this chapter. The fact is this: There is a vital relationship between the Christian faith and healing. I have discovered a five-fold relationship.

1. To begin with, the Christian faith inspires healthy living and this is the best prevention of disease. Just suppose an individual from his early life really lived the Christian way — would not healthy living result in most instances and much sickness be avoided?

Dr. James Van Buskirk in his volume Religion, Healing and Health, reminds us that there are nine characteristics of the Christian way of life, all of which contribute to a person's health. Christianity teaches and encourages the proper care of the body. It enforces the virtue of honest work, which has a definite therapeutic value. The Christian Faith promotes recreation and relaxation. It encourages a person to turn from himself and to rest in the Lord. Christianity encourages Christian worship, which also has a therapeutic effect. It encourages the study of the Bible, which becomes a marvelous opportunity for the constructive power of suggestion to operate upon the personality. The Christian Gospel offers faith as the only antidote to fear; and it frees the human personality from the devastating burden of guilt. Jesus Christ always says "forgive," "love one another."

2. There is a second relationship between the Christian faith and healing. The Christian faith is able to aid healing through physical and psychological methods by the creation of the proper mental, emotional, and spiritual attitudes within the patient. Just as healing through physical methods is impeded by wrong mental, emotional, and spiritual attitudes, it is aided by right attitudes. This is clearly demonstrated in what is commonly known as "the will to live." Negatively considered, there are case records to what are called "psychological deaths." There are patients who lose interest in life, and feeling that there is nothing worth living for, they succumb to the first illness that comes along.

And even when death does not result, the process of physical and mental recovery is impeded drastically and prolonged by wrong attitudes toward life. A noted doctor once told of the surprisingly slow recovery of a female patient after a mild attack of influenza. Even though there was no physical cause for her continuing debility, she continued to have no appetite, a poor pulse, and to look unfit. Finally, it was discovered that the reason she was failing to recover normally was because she did not want to recover. If she recovered, she knew she would have to return to a job, which was causing her much unhappiness.

Positively speaking, it is this "will to live" which is often the deciding factor between death and recovery. An anesthetist said: "patients who go for the operating table with a confident faith in God take less anesthetic, recover from it more easily and with far less of the usual distressing aftereffects."

3. To make the analysis complete, there is a third relationship that should be mentioned. There have been times when the Church's ministry of healing and medical science have joined hands to effect a healing, each contributing

something to the healing, that the other could not contribute. There is the record of the young boy in South Africa who needed a brain operation, but was subject to blackouts. The brain surgeon in Johannesburg said that he could not operate until the boy had been free of blackouts for six months. In desperation the parents took their son to Mrs. Elsie Salmon, the wife of a Methodist minister, who has had a remarkable ministry of healing. After eight months, the boy had experienced no blackouts. They returned him to the surgeon in Johannesburg. The operation was performed. It was one of the earliest operations on record where they removed a sphere of the brain. The operation was a success. Now what had happened? The Church's ministry of healing did something and medical science did something. Together, they contributed to healing. I predict that this is going to be a rapidly developing relationship.

4. We come now to the fourth relationship between the Christian faith and healing. The Christian faith is able to heal all those functional illnesses, which have been caused by wrong mental, emotional, or spiritual attitudes. A functional illness is one in which there is nothing wrong with the organs or structure of the body, but the organs or the structure are malfunctioning because of wrong attitudes or emotions within the person. Doctors estimate conservatively that 75% of all illnesses are functional.

How devastating is the effect of destructive emotions upon the body and the mind. Every negative emotion, except the normal expression of grief, is destructive. Such things as fear, anxiety, ill will, guilt, inferiority, negativism are destructive in their effect upon the human personality.

Dr. Blaine E. McLaughlen, director of psychiatry at Women's Medical College, Philadelphia, says that 60% to 85% of all patients in doctor's offices have psychosomatic complaints. He says that 99% of all headaches, 75% of all gastric upsets, 75% of all skin disease, and 85% of all asthma causes are psychosomatic in nature.

A heart specialist in Fredericksburg, Virginia, said: "85% of people with heart conditions have nothing structurally wrong with them...the disturbance is functional. Fear is the great trouble. I have to spend most of my time telling people they have nothing structurally wrong with them."

A doctor who attended the medical needs of a General Motors plant in a certain city said: "75% of the executives of this plant have gastric ulcers due to the pressures upon them to succeed or be replaced."

Dr. Karl Menninger says: "Guilt changes the physical structure of the body and makes the person more susceptible to disease."

In December, 1964, Dr. John W. Keyes, a heart specialist of the Henry Ford Hospital in Detroit, Michigan, speaking at a scientific meeting of the American Medical Association in Miami Beach, Florida, declared that some heart disease may be imaginary, brought on by the patient's fears and his doctor's words or attitudes. Dr. Keyes explained: "The patients may have symptoms ranging from chest pains to dizziness, from fatigue to palpitations. Once symptoms of this type have occurred, they of themselves can produce a vicious cycle of anxiety which convinces the patient that heart disease is actually present."

It would appear that the only way to deal with these functional illnesses is to deal with the cause of them, and the cause is a negative emotion. The only way to get rid of a negative emotion is to put into its place a positive emotion. The only way to replace a negative emotion by a positive emotion is through the power of Jesus Christ in the disciplined conscious life and the work of the Holy Spirit in the subconscious.

5. The final aspect of the relationship between the Christian faith and healing is healing by the direct activity of God apart from the use of intermediary psychological or physical methods. Human experience bears eloquent testimony to healing by the direct touch of after human skill has been unable to go any further, after physical and psychological methods have exhausted themselves. When we speak of healing by the direct activity of God apart from the use of intermediary psychological or physical methods, we refer to God intervening directly in a person's experience, apart from all recognizable human sources of remedy and cure, bringing to that individual healing that is clearly demonstrable, at the place of the mind, or soul, or body, or in a combination of any two of these areas of human personality, or of all three areas.

The testimonies to such Divine healings, which have been scientifically confirmed, are innumerable. These would comprise a separate study, impossible within the limits of this chapter.

Fact 4
.....

There is a fourth fact that is compelling. There has never been a time when so many people need some kind of healing. As I move among people, I am distressed by the lack of radiance in the spirit of many people. Individuals seem burdened and bored. In the faces and attitudes of people there is evidence of insecurity and fear. I am convinced that this lack of radiance in the personality of people is due to the need for some kind of inward healing.

I also find everywhere people who are unusually tired. Some time ago there appeared in a national weekly an article entitled, "Why Are Half of Us So Tired?" The author commented on the contemporary situation in these words: "'Beat' – 'bushed' – 'pooped,' or just plain 'dead' – no matter how they express it, millions of Americans complain of various degrees of fatigue." He goes on to quote a medical doctor who reported that "at least 50% of the adults I see say they are tired."

One of the major types of chronic fatigue is psychological. Such a fatigue has been described as "an illness due to being caught in a trap." E. Stanley Jones lists nine psychological and spiritual causes and tiredness: self-centeredness, boredom, worry, fear, inferiority feelings, resentments, indecisions, oversensitivity, and inner guilts. All such causes require healing within the person.

Then consider all the nervous illness in the world. It has been said that nervous maladies are probably responsible for more mental and physical suffering than any other category of disease.

What about the vast amount of mental sickness? It has been estimated recently that one in every ten Americans is suffering from a mental or emotional disorder. Mental patients occupy about half of all hospital beds in the United States. Each year 250,000 more patients enter mental hospitals. Approximately one-half of those rejected for military service suffer from some kind of mental disturbance or emotional maladjustment.

Mental sickness is becoming a major problem in American industry. Dr. William C. Menninger, a psychiatrist whose career centered around the study of mental health problems in business and industry, said: "From 60% to 80% to technical incompetence."

In one General Motors plant of 5,800 employees, psychiatric and psychological problems were found in more than half of the workers reporting for medical care; most were made physically ill by those emotional problems. The Wall Street Journal, which calls mental illness "industry's top medical problem," notes that emotional problems figure prominently in the estimated twelve billion dollar loss which American industry suffers each year in absenteeism, employee turnover, alcoholism, industrial accidents, and lowered productivity caused by friction between workers. Today approximately 500 psychiatrists devote part or all of their time as consultants to companies sponsoring mental health programs.

Consider the prevalence of physical illness. Hospitals everywhere are crowded beyond normal capacity. In a recent year, nearly one million more persons were admitted to hospitals in the United States than the preceding year. In the U.S.A. only one in every five persons enjoys optimum health. During a recent year sickness cost the American people the staggering sum of 58 billion dollars.

And how tragic is the spiritual sickness everywhere evident. There is a declining sense of respect for authority and acts of lawlessness are increasing phenomenally. The old immorality has become the new morality. Purity is now considered a vice, not a virtue. Men are separated from their fellows and alienated from God. Nothing other than the healing of "the balm of Gilead," effected at the Cross of Christ, can suffice.

Fact 5
. . . . .

Let me state, in the briefest terms, a final compelling fact. Every day miracles of healing are occurring and many of them are being witnessed to in our experience. Read the newspapers, the healing magazines, and the books in the field. Talk with those active in healing ministries. Attend conferences where the healed gather. Miracles of healing are being confirmed as actualities.

Some time ago I tried a simple experiment. One week hence I was to give a message on healing. I made a study of healing information that came to me unsolicited each day. The result was that every day during that week I received evidence of at least one new miracle of healing. I have been a student of all participants in the Church's ministry of healing since 1951. The evidence of the reality of healings, through such a ministry, is cumulative. Everywhere healings are occurring – if we only have eyes to see.

Here, then, are Five Facts That Are Compelling. Jesus, as a religious leader, inaugurated a ministry of healing. In the Early Christian Church healing was a regular ministry. There is a vital relationship between the Christian faith and healing. There was never a time when so many people needed some kind of healing. Every day miracles of healing are being witnessed before our very eyes.

What is our relationship to such compelling facts? It seems to be that we are compelled, first of all, to come to a reasonable conclusion concerning the validity of Christian healing. Secondly, I believe that we are impelled to participate in the Church's ministry of healing. And certainly we are motivated to become persistent and persuasive witnesses to the reality of the spiritual realm and of Christian healing within a world, which is too often blinded by naturalistic concepts and too often confined in its low-vaulted prison house of materialistic activity.

The Healing Steps
• • • • • • • • •

God's healing, through any of the healing methods, is to be sought along a clearly marked path. There are definite healing steps to be taken by the person seeking healing.

The first step is that of Relaxation. "Be still and know that I am God," (Psalm 46:10). In seeking healing, the body must be relaxed and freed of all tension. In fact, the body must be "forgotten" so that the mind can concentrate on God and on His healing power. The mind must also be relaxed. Just as the sky cannot be reflected on troubled waters, so the presence of God cannot be realized by a restless spirit.

The Second step is that of Purging. "If we walk in the light as he is in the light, we have fellowship one with another, and the blood of Jesus Christ his Son cleanseth us from all sin," (1 John 1:7). The subconscious mind must be cleansed of all wrong emotions and sinful states, so that the healing power of God can flow through it. There must be the consciousness of divine forgiveness in the soul. God's healing power can work only in those who are living in accord with His laws. A person must rid himself of anything and everything that would keep God from working effectively in his life.

The third step is that of Clarification. "And Jesus stood still and called them, and said, What will ye that I shall do unto you?" (Matthew 20:32). A person must be specific, not general, in his request for healing. He must visualize exactly his need and vocalize his desire. He must tell God exactly what he is seeking. The person seeking healing must not be vague.

The fourth step is that of Consecration. "Whether we live therefore, or die, we are the Lord's," (Romans 14:8). One of the conditions of divine healing is this spiritual attitude of the absolute relinquishment of one's life to the will of God. There must be complete surrender to God on the part of the one seeking divine healing. If the will of God be that health is restored immediately, then let God be praised. If health cannot be restored at once, then let the seeker realize that God is in every human circumstance and that ultimately His purpose will be made manifest. Just so, the seeker must be characterized by a sincere willingness to glorify God and to live for others. Healing, when received, cannot be hoarded selfishly. The renewed strength and the restored health are to be dedicated to God for the blessing and the service of one's fellow men.

The fifth step, and indeed a strategic step, is that of Anticipation. That is the step of faith. "Faith is the substance of things hoped for, the evidence of things not seen," (Hebrews 11:1). As one seeks healing there must be an eager expectancy, and attitude of an active faith. Never must a seeker think in terms of failure. Always there is the anticipation of God fulfilling what He has already promised. Just as a person must be specific as he visualizes his need for healing, so must he be able to visualize himself as healed in the particular area of need when his prayer is answered.

Faith for healing involves the use of the imagination. Like every other faculty the Christian's imagination should be sanctified. Such a sanctified imagination in its relation to healing demands that one should sustain in imagination only pictures of God at work in his body; annihilating germs, subduing, toxins, repairing diseased tissues. Lightfoot's translation of Hebrews 11:1 suggests that "faith is that which gives reality to things hoped for."

One of the chief obstacles in healing is the "old mindset," the preoccupation with disease or some habitual notion about its incurability, or some stubbornness of opinion which, once having denied the possibility of spiritual healing, is reluctant to admit its error. God is equally helpless before the negatives of both intellectual doubt and negative imaginations.

Thus, in seeking healing, there must be the spirit of anticipation.

The final step is that of Appropriation. "I can do all things through Christ which strengtheneth me," (Philippians 4:13). The seeker receives what God has promised, begins acting in the strength of the healing power received, and is grateful to God for the reality of the healing power in his life. "Father, I thank thee," is the consummation of the personal appropriation of the divine blessings.

A Remarkable Healing

• • • • • • • • •

George Mamoru Nakajima was a student at Asbury Theological Seminary 1961-65. He was born in Okayama, Japan, and was graduated forrm Osaka Christian College and Osaka Theological Seminary. After a two-year pastorate in Japan, he entered Asbury Theological Seminary, and was graduated in 1965.

During his senior year at Asbury Theological Seminary George Nakajima experienced a marvelous healing. The thrilling story of his healing is presented below, as it was related to me by George. May it thrill you as it has thrilled all of us at Asbury Theological Seminary.

One Sunday night after returning home from conducting a meeting in the church of a friend in Ohio, I discovered that I was bleeding inwardly. By the time I was admitted to the Good Samaritan Hospital in Lexington, Kentucky, I had lost two-thirds of my blood and was terribly weak.

I spent nine weeks in the hospital and had three major operations upon my stomach and intestines. Such operations took from three to four hours. Even though I had three operations on my intestines before coming to this country, this recent hospital experience was to have the most meaning for me, both physically and spiritually.

I have been healed and have returned to my studies at Asbury Theological Seminary. My healing is due to the prayers of many friends, both known and unknown. Of course, God used brilliant doctors, excellent hospital equipment and highly developed medical science. But there are many things about my healing that cannot be explained even by the doctors. My doctor told one of my friends that my case was a miracle.

One week after the first operation in the Lexington hospital, my small intestine became blocked and I had severe pain. The doctors then performed the second operation on me, working four hours. But even after the operation, things did not go well. Food would not pass through me. So, ten days after the second operation I had a third operation. Even after this I was kept on the critical list because I was not eating and was extremely weak. I could not even digest liquids.

These weeks in the hospital were significant to me spiritually. Physically I suffered much. But I also gained spiritual victories. Each one of the operations confronted me with a spiritual crisis. At the time of the first operation, I prayed for God's help because I worried about my family, my school program, my finances, etc. But I was so selfish in my praying.

At the time of the second operation, I prayed because I was afraid. I was afraid of the suffering, because I had suffered so much after the first operation. Ironically, the second operation was hardest of the three.

I remember the day before the third operation. I prayed sincerely: "Lord, forgive me. I was wrong. I was so selfish. I do not know whether I can make it this time because I am so weak. But I know one thing, I need peace. Give me Thy peace, and Thy will be done." I remember that immediately wonderful peace came into my heart. Fear and worry were gone, and my heart was so calm. I praised and thanked God.

The third operation took more than four hours. But as I awakened in the recovery room I had peace and not as much pain as before. This victory of faith was a wonderful experience.

A week later, pain came back. My doctor came to me and said, "George, maybe we will have to operate again. If so, it may take all day." I prayed again "Thy will be done."

It was at this time that the idea of a special healing service was suggested to me by my pastor, the Revered Clyde Van Valin. He helped to prepare me for the healing service.

Within a short time, three men of God — my pastor; Mr. John Fitch, a layman; and the President of the Seminary — came to my room for the healing service. They anointed me, laid hands on me, and prayed for my healing.

During the healing service, the President of the Seminary reminded me of the healing steps. I was really impressed by his statement that faith must have some imagination in it. He said, "imagine yourself healed by God and for the glory of God." I immediately imagined myself healed by God and back in Japan witnessing to my own people.

I want to testify that from the time of the healing service in my hospital room I began to recover. I amazed the doctors. There was no fourth operation. My meals were increased little by little. My body began to function much more normally.

I returned to my home. Now I am back in theological seminary. I have been healed by the mercy and power of God.

I have rededicated my whole life to God for His glory. Jesus is not only the Savior of my soul but also the Healer of my body. I love Him because He loves me and holds me in His hand. My faith as well as my health has been renewed. When I have finished seminary I will carry the glad tidings of salvation to my own people in Japan.

George Nakajima

Since his Asbury Theological Seminary days George has had both an intensive and extensive ministry. For a time he combined teaching and pastoral work in a western city. Since his return to Japan he is busily engaged in both the teaching ministry and the work of evangelism. George never ceases to praise God for his supernatural healing.

www.ingramcontent.com/pod-product-compliance
Lightning Source LLC
Chambersburg PA
CBHW030010040426
42337CB00012BA/720